A Faculty and Staff Guide to
Creating Learning Outcomes

Jimmie Gahagan, John Dingfelder, and Katharine Pei

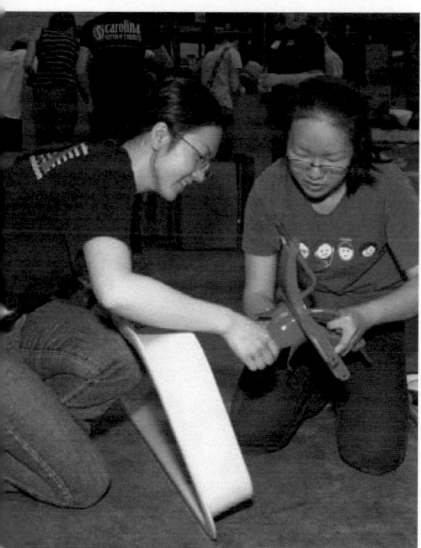

NATIONAL RESOURCE CENTER
FIRST-YEAR EXPERIENCE® AND STUDENTS IN TRANSITION
UNIVERSITY OF SOUTH CAROLINA

We would like to thank the following institutions for providing photographs for the guide:

Southeast Missouri State University pp. 5, 8, 11, 15, 22; University of South Carolina cover, pp. 7, 13, 14, 25

Copyright © 2010 University of South Carolina. All rights reserved. No part of this work may be reproduced or copied in any form, by any means, without written permission of the University of South Carolina.

ISBN 978-1-889-27167-5

The First-Year Experience® is a service mark of the University of South Carolina. A license may be granted upon written request to use the term "The First-Year Experience. " This license is not transferable without written approval of the University of South Carolina.

Production Staff for the National Resource Center:

Project Manager	Tracy L. Skipper, Assistant Director for Publications
Project Editor	Emily Mullins, Editorial Assistant
Design and Production	Angie Mellor, Graphic Artist

Additional copies of this guide may be obtained from the National Resource Center for The First-Year Experience and Students in Transition, University of South Carolina, 1728 College Street, Columbia, SC 29208. Telephone (803) 777-6229. Fax (803) 777-4699.

Contents

About This Guide 7

What Is Assessment? 8

What Are Learning Outcomes? 11

Why Use Learning Outcomes? 12

A Model for Creating Learning Outcomes 13

Format of the Learning Outcome Statement . . 15

Assessing Learning Outcomes 20

Concluding Thoughts 27

Assessment Resources 28

References 28

About the Authors 30

Demonstrating student learning has become increasingly important for faculty and administrators at all levels of higher education. Now more than ever, we are being asked to show the value of the college experience and describe the tangible benefits and competencies associated with degree completion. Developing measurable learning outcomes is the first step in the assessment process, and, when done well, it not only guides our methodology but also dramatically improves our work with students in and beyond the classroom.

This publication is designed to encourage faculty and staff to create, use, and assess measurable learning outcomes in and outside the classroom. For those educators not familiar with creating learning outcomes, this guide provides a brief overview of assessment and a starting place for creating and measuring meaningful learning outcomes. For those more familiar with learning outcomes, we challenge you to use this guide to examine those outcomes currently associated with the courses, programs, and initiatives you facilitate and consider how these might be made more useful for program administrators, faculty, and students. Regardless of your expertise, we believe this guide can be most helpful when readers take time to examine their own practice and, through meaningful reflection, make changes to improve student learning and engagement. Therefore, we encourage you to use the workbook format and questions for reflection to help you in this process.

About This Guide

The beginning of this guide provides a brief overview of the nature and importance of assessment. Next, we define learning outcomes and offer specific recommendations for creating them. We then discuss strategies for assessing learning outcomes and conclude with resources you can use to further your understanding of this topic.

In this guide, we encourage readers to use the Bloom's revised taxonomy (Anderson & Krathwohl, 2001) as outlined on page 13. This model is flexible and allows educators the ability to adapt it to the language associated with their specific discipline or field. As Anderson and Krathwohl describe, "there has always been and remains to this day an expectation that the taxonomy would be adapted as educators in different fields used it, as education changed, and as new knowledge provided a basis for change" (p. xxviii). The revised taxonomy is straightforward and easy-to-use, making it especially valuable for faculty and staff who are new to learning outcomes assessment. We recognize that other models for creating learning outcomes have been developed, and so as you become more familiar with using Bloom's revised taxonomy, we encourage you to also explore other models (see, for example, Hannah & Michaelis, 1977; Hauenstein, 1998; Marzano & Kendall, 2008).

Throughout the guide, readers will find Questions for Reflection and Questions for Reflection and Practice. These are designed to help you begin to think about the assessment process and the relationship of specific learning outcomes to larger institutional, program, or course goals. By working through these prompts, readers should walk away from this guide with specific learning outcomes for their course or program, a strategy for measuring progress toward achieving that outcome, and a plan for how assessment results will be used to improve future student performance and/or the program itself.

"Assessment is a set of processes designed to improve, demonstrate, and inquire about student learning." (Mentkowski qtd. in Bresciani, Zelna, & Anderson, 2004, p. 1)

What Is Assessment?

Upcraft and Schuh (1996) define assessment as "any effort to gather, analyze, and interpret evidence which describes institutional, departmental, divisional, or agency effectiveness" (p. 18). However, systematic assessment efforts are likely to yield more timely and useful results.

Astin's (1993) I-E-O model serves as an ideal framework for designing learning outcomes and an overall assessment plan. Learning does not occur in a vacuum, and to properly assess a course or program, educators must take into account individual learner characteristics and situational factors. Astin's model attempts to account for these factors in measuring the impact of educational initiatives. As Figure 1 shows, inputs, environment, and outcomes are interlinked. If a component is left out, the assessment may be incomplete or inaccurate. For example, if we fail to account for students' current performance level on a task, we are unable to comment on whether their achievement of a learning outcome related to that task has changed. As Schuh, Upcraft, and Associates (2001) note, "Only when both inputs and experiences are taken into account may one explain a particular [outcome]" (p. 154).

Figure 1. Astin's (1993) I-E-O Model offers a framework for assessment planning.

Input variables are the characteristics that a student brings with him or her, such as gender, race, GPA, educational background, financial status, and choice of major (Astin, 1993). These can also be thought of as control, pretest, or predictor variables. Environmental variables include anything that happens during the program, event, or academic course that may have an impact on the student. Examples include the instructor, program facilitator, teaching style, the facility, interactions with peers, place of residence, or cocurricular experiences (Astin). Outcomes "refer to the 'talents' we are trying to develop in our educational program"(Astin, p. 18). An outcome might be retention, degree completion rates, test or assignment grades, overall course or program satisfaction, postcollege aspirations, or GPA (Astin). These might also be thought of as dependent or posttest variables.

The I-E-O model is useful when writing learning outcomes because it helps educators account for student inputs, such as preparedness, as they enter the course or program. For example, if the previous science course experience of students enrolled in a chemistry class ranges from none to four or five courses, it may be unrealistic to expect every student to memorize all elements on the periodic table in a single academic term. Instead, instructors may need to write a learning outcome to measure the learning of each individual student with the expectation that most of them will be able to recall 15 more elements on the periodic table than they knew prior to enrolling in the course.

It is also important to take into account environmental factors when assessing learning outcomes. For example, a group of students who live on a residence hall floor together might be expected to identify three ways to confront their roommates about a disagreement. However, if the resident assistant of a particular floor quits suddenly, and no floor meetings were held during the first semester, it is unlikely those students would be able to meet the expected learning outcome. There is an environmental factor that led to them not meeting the outcome. If an assessment of the entire building demonstrated that students largely achieved this outcome with the exception of residents on one floor, having information about this environmental factor would be helpful in interpreting the results.

Questions for Reflection

What is my course or program supposed to accomplish? What kinds of outcomes do I desire for our students?

What strategies are currently in place to help me achieve these outcomes?

What do I know about the students who enter my course or program?

What, if anything, am I currently doing to measure progress toward desired outcomes?

How might my current methods need to be changed to give me a more complete picture of how students move toward these desired outcomes?

What environmental factors may have influenced student performance?

"Using and understanding assessment results will encourage important dialogue about the mission of educational institutions and how well the intended outcomes of higher education are being achieved by our joint efforts to facilitate student learning and development." (Hanson qtd. in Bresciani, Zelna, & Anderson, 2004, p. vii)

What Are Learning Outcomes?

Developing measurable learning outcomes is a first step in assessing student learning. Creating outcomes that are specific to the skills and/or knowledge we would like our students to obtain is crucial in achieving the larger institutional course or program objectives. However, as opposed to broader mission and course description statements, learning outcomes are specific, measurable objectives that describe what an individual will learn and be able to do as a result of a lesson or program. The downward flow from mission/course description statements to learning outcomes provides students with the purpose of the course or activity being experienced.

Characteristics of Learning Outcomes

Learning outcomes

- Express what the student will be able to know or do
- Focus on the product rather than the process
- Are measurable (i.e., identifiable or observable)
- Are detailed and specific (whereas goals are broad and general)
- Include action verbs such as define, compare, create, design, or develop (See Figure 3 for a more exhaustive list; Bresciani, Zelna, & Anderson, 2004.)

Why Use Learning Outcomes?

As in life, setting goals and objectives both in and beyond the classroom encourage us to stay focused on the particular task ahead and the type of learning that we want to occur. Students perform at a higher level and can become more self-guided when we articulate our expectations through learning outcomes. They help us prioritize the techniques and learning experiences that will be most effective in our work with students and can guide curriculum decisions. Having learning outcomes in place also makes it easier to check for understanding and skills or competencies achieved by our students both in and out of the classroom. They can also provide a bridge to connect student learning in and/or beyond the classroom with institutional mission and goal statements. Finally, we focus on learning outcomes because they have become increasingly important in the areas of assessment, accreditation, and accountability within higher education. As Bresciani et al. (2004) remind us, a focus on learning outcomes allows us to not "only speak with confidence about 'what we do' but . . . also discuss 'how well we do it'" (p. 1).

■ Questions for Reflection

Why am I creating learning outcomes?

_____

_____

_____

_____

Which, if any, key institutional statements, descriptions, and/or goals support the development of learning outcomes in my context?

_____

_____

_____

_____

A Model for Creating Learning Outcomes

The Taxonomy of Educational Objectives, created by Benjamin Bloom and David Krathwohl in the 1950s, is a means of expressing qualitatively different kinds of thinking (Bloom, 1956). Bloom's Taxonomy has since been adapted for classroom use as a planning tool and continues to be one of the most universally applied models across all levels of schooling and in all areas of study. Bloom's initial framework places greater emphasis on the cognitive aspects of learning. As our understanding of student development theory and cognitive psychology grew over the years, the need to revise Bloom's original taxonomy became evident (Anderson & Krathwohl, 2001).

During the 1990s, Lorin Anderson, a former student of Benjamin Bloom and Carolina Distinguished Professor Emeritus at the University of South Carolina, and David Krathwohl,

> "... because complex learning is a goal of higher education it is important to create learning outcomes that challenge students to emerge from their embeddedness by connecting to their cognitive, interpersonal, and intrapersonal dimensions of development." (Komives & Shoper, 2004, p. 28)

Professor Emeritus at Syracuse University, led a team of cognitive psychologists in revising the taxonomy to examine its relevance as we entered the 21st century (Overbaugh & Schultz, 2008). Anderson and Krathwohl's team expanded Bloom's original taxonomy by adding types of learning to create a two-dimensional model that focused on both the knowledge domain and cognitive process. As Anderson and Krathwohl (2001) described, there are four types of knowledge: factual, conceptual, procedural, and metacognitive. These four categories "are designed to reflect the intermediate level of specificity associated with educational objectives" and help "educators distinguish what to teach" (Anderson & Krathwohl, p. 39). For example, if faculty or staff want to educate students about diversity, one of the first steps would be to identify the type of knowledge most appropriate for the course or activity. Should students be able to recall facts or identify key concepts of diversity, or should they be able to connect these facts to more complex issues addressed? The answers to these questions will determine what level of knowledge is most appropriate.

> "Learning is not merely academic or cognitive learning; it is a transformative process including affective development and identity."
> (Komives & Shoper, 2004, p. 28)

Next, Anderson and Krathwohl (2001) describe six categories or levels of cognitive process that include remembering, understanding, applying, analyzing, evaluating, and creating (Figure 2). As faculty and staff create learning outcomes, the topic and level of knowledge associated with the desired outcome will help guide the selection of the most appropriate cognitive process. In this framework, the levels of cognitive process build on one another. When creating learning outcomes, educators should consider writing outcomes that span the full range of cognitive processes: "assessment tasks should tap cognitive processes that go beyond remembering…these tasks can (and often should) be supplemented with those that tap the full range of cognitive processes required for the transfer of learning" (Anderson & Krathwohl, p. 91). Again using the example of diversity, if one objective of the course or program is to have students gain a factual comprehension of the topic, then emphasizing the cognitive process of remembering by asking students if they are able to recognize or recall key facts would be appropriate.

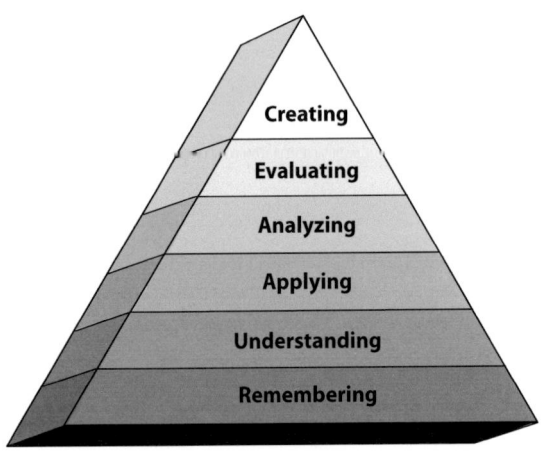

Figure 2. Bloom's Revised Taxonomy (Overbaugh & Schultz, 2008). Reprinted with permission.

When developing educational outcomes, it is also important to consider that learning is not strictly a cognitive process; rather, students' environment, background, and psychomotor development, along with other factors, play a role in shaping their learning. Therefore, when creating learning outcomes, educators should not only consider the level of cognitive process in which they are asking students to engage and to the type of knowledge necessary for the course or program but also the specific developmental frameworks within which students may be operating. Relevant student development theories include Chickering and Reisser's (1993) theory of psychosocial development, Cross's (1991) model of racial identity development, and theories of cognitive-structural development (Baxter-Magolda, 1992; King & Kitchener, 1994; Perry, 1970). While a discussion of these theories is beyond the scope of this guide, educators are encouraged to consider how students' psychosocial and intellectual development may impact their ability to achieve particular learning outcomes.

Format of the Learning Outcome Statement

Bloom's Revised Taxonomy establishes a guide for developing programmatic and course-level learning outcomes. At its essence, each learning outcome is described by a sentence that consists of an action verb related to a cognitive process and clearly defined content related to a specific knowledge type (Center for Teaching Excellence, 2009).

All learning outcomes have a common format:

    Subject - Verb - Object

The Subject of the Learning Outcome Statement

The SUBJECT of the learning outcome statement is the student or the learner (Center for Teaching Excellence, 2009).

- The *student* will...
- *Students* will...
- The *student* should...
- *Students* should...

Photo: Southeast Missouri State University

The Object of the Learning Outcome Statement

The OBJECT of the learning outcome statement is the skill or content knowledge the educator is addressing as a part of the program or course. For example, one object of a learning outcome statement for a first-year seminar might be "students' knowledge of specific campus resources." Again, object statements are specific to the content being addressed in a particular course or program. As Anderson and Krathwohl (2001) described, object statements generally fall into four categories of knowledge: factual, conceptual, procedural, and metacognitive.

The Verb of the Learning Outcome Statement

The VERB in learning outcome statements is connected to specific cognitive processes (Figure 3).

Levels of Cognitive Process	Action Verbs
Remembering Can the student recall or remember the information?	Define, duplicate, list, memorize, recall, repeat, reproduce, state
Understanding Can the student explain ideas or concepts?	Classify, describe, discuss, explain, identify, locate, recognize, report, select, translate, paraphrase
Applying Can the student use the information in a new way?	Choose, dramatize, demonstrate, employ, illustrate, interpret, operate, schedule, sketch, solve, use, write
Analyzing Can the student distinguish between the different parts?	Appraise, argue, compare, criticize, differentiate, discriminate, distinguish, examine, experiment, question, test
Evaluating Can the student justify a position or decision?	Appraise, argue, judge, defend, select, support, value, evaluate
Creating Can the student create a new product or point of view?	Assemble, construct, create, design, develop, formulate, write

Figure 3. Action verbs associated with cognitive processes in Bloom's Revised Taxonomy. (Adapted from Anderson & Krathwohl, 2001, p. 31).

The Taxonomy Table (Figure 4) brings together both the learning outcome verb (cognitive process) and a knowledge type (broad classification for course content) to describe a specific outcome. For example, an outcome from a first-year seminar course could be to explain the connection between students' service-learning experience and their transition to the university. The object of this statement is "the connection between the students' service-learning experience and their transition to the university." This object describes self-knowledge, which, in Anderson and Krathwohl's (2001) framework, falls under metacognitive knowledge. The verb in this statement, "to explain," falls under the cognitive process of understanding. Therefore, this outcome would be located under 2D.

Another example could be that as a result of engaging in the judicial process, students will describe how they will be held accountable for violations of the code of conduct. The object in this statement is "how they will be held accountable for violations," which is procedural knowledge. The verb "describe" implies understanding from the student; therefore, this outcome would fall under 2C.

	The Cognitive Process Dimension					
The Knowledge Dimension	1. Remember	2. Understand	3. Apply	4. Analyze	5. Evaluate	6. Create
A. Factual Knowledge	1A	2A	3A	4A	5A	6A
B. Conceptual Knowledge	1B	2B	3B	4B	5B	6B
C. Procedural Knowledge	1C	2C	3C	4C	5C	6C
D. Metacognitive Knowledge	1D	2D	3D	4D	5D	6D

Figure 4. Cognitive process and knowledge dimension matrix for Bloom's Revised Taxonomy.

Note. From *A Taxonomy for Learning, Teaching, and Assessing: A Revision of Bloom's Taxonomy of Educational Objectives* (p. 28), by L. W. Anderson and D. R. Krathwonl, 2001, New York: Addison Wesley Longman. Copyright 2001 by Pearson Education, Inc. Reprinted with permission.

Examples of Learning Outcomes

Below are additional examples of learning outcomes that apply the Revised Bloom's Taxonomy to learning experiences in and out of the classroom.

Remembering:

Example **Course**: The student will be able to list the four stages of group development (1B).

Program: The orientation leader will be able to recall campus resources for incoming first-year students (1A).

Understanding:

Example **Course**: The student will be able to describe and discuss the final moments that ended the Battle of Gettysburg (2B).

Program: The student will be able to identify three ways to confront roommate disagreements (2D).

Applying:

Example **Course**: The student will be able to demonstrate the flow of waste water from point A to point B using a diagram drawn to scale (3C).

Program: The student will be able to illustrate one significant event that impacted his or her experience while at the art gallery (3D).

Analyzing:

Example **Course**: The student will be able to compare three pros and three cons of a national healthcare system in the United States (4A).

Program: The resident will be able to examine and compare his/her beliefs to those of his or her suitemates (4D).

Evaluating:

Example **Course**: The student will be able to defend his or her position on government policies related to the national deficit (5B).

Program: The student will be able to evaluate his or her university's admissions process (5C).

Creating:

Example **Course**: The student will be able to design a plan for revitalizing a failing downtown area (6D).

Program: The students will be able to create a new mission statement for their organization (6D).

Questions for Reflection and Practice

What are the mission(s); general education outcomes; and institutional, departmental, or unit goals that will influence specific learning outcomes for my course or program?

_____

_____

_____

What kind of knowledge do I want the student to gain from the course, event, or experience?

Example **Course:** Accounting 101 – Basic accounting skills

Students gain *procedural knowledge* and are able to apply specific accounting methods and procedures.

Program: Day-long community service event – Activity that serves the area community

Students gain *metacognitive knowledge* and are able to self-reflect, learning more about themselves and the importance of being a citizen of the world.

_____

_____

_____

What level of cognitive process do I want students to reach within that knowledge domain?

Example **Accounting 101:** Applying
Community Service: Understanding

_____

_____

_____

Write a learning outcome that reflects the knowledge students will achieve and the process by which they will achieve it.

Example **Accounting 101:** At the end of the course, students will…

Be able to interpret debit and credit transactions

Be able to prepare accurate financial statements

Community Service: As a result of participating in this event, students will…

Recognize their ability to make a positive contribution to the community

Describe the needs of the local community

_____

_____

_____

_____

_____

_____

Assessing Learning Outcomes

Learning outcomes are only useful if they are assessed. Program and course improvement occurs only after evaluating what strategies (e.g., teaching, facilitation, activities, assignments) were successful and deciding how to capitalize on those strengths to improve future courses and programs. This section provides information on how to assess learning outcomes.

When assessing learning outcomes, it is important to be realistic. For example, it may not be feasible to capture qualitative assessment data for all or most participants in large-scale classes or events. In those cases, selecting a sample of participants to complete an open-ended survey or participate in focus groups may be more feasible. Because multiple people may be teaching or facilitating a class or event and because students do not experience courses or events in a vacuum, educators will also need to consider how they will control or account for the impact of environmental variables.

It is also important to know individual limitations in regard to conducting assessment. Where educators do not have a strong knowledge base of survey design, qualitative methodology, or statistical analysis, they may need to seek out faculty and staff colleagues in institutional research or psychology, statistics, or education departments as assessment partners.

Finally, it is important to know how assessment data will be used before they are collected. If the results will be widely disseminated, information that might identify individual students or class sections would need to be removed from final reports. Moreover, educators need to consider the audience for the assessment results and which kinds of information will be most useful for their purposes.

Types of Assessment

There are two types of assessment: direct and indirect. Direct assessment "involves looking at actual samples of student work produced in our programs"(Skidmore College, 2009, para. 1) and measures actual student learning, activity, or ability. Indirect assessment is the process of "gathering information through means other than looking at actual samples of student work" (Skidmore College, 2009, para. 2) and measures perceptions or opinions of the learner (Bosland, 2007; Skidmore College, 2009). Examples of each type of assessment and how they can be used for both course-based and programmatic-based assessment can be found in Figures 5 and 6.

Course-based assessment most often uses direct assessment, either through quantitative or qualitative exams or the evaluation of student work through an assignment. Programmatic-based assessment may come in the form of either direct or indirect assessment. Figure 5 offers an overview of direct and indirect assessment measures.

Direct	Indirect
Standardized tests: Instructors provide direct assessment of student learning through • Tests/quizzes • Papers • Course assignments • Presentations • Performances • Simulations • Electronic portfolios • Capstone projects	*Surveys:* Student surveys/evaluations • End-of-course evaluations Satisfaction surveys • Student • Alumni • Employer Pre-post surveys • Change in perception over time *Qualitative data:* • In-class group discussions • Focus groups • Exit interviews *Institutional data:* • Participation in activities • Honors, awards, scholarships, fellowships earned • Time to degree • Postgraduation employment placement rates • Course progression and completion

Figure 5. Examples of direct and indirect assessment measures. (Anderson & Krathwohl, 2001; Bosland, 2007; Center for Teaching Excellence, 2009; Miami Dade College, 2004; Skidmore College, 2009)

Photo: Southeast Missouri State University

"Assessment is not an end in itself but a vehicle for organizational effectiveness."
(Upcraft & Schuh, 1996, p. 22)

Figure 6 provides examples of both course-based and programmatic assessment formats as they relate to each level of knowledge in Bloom's Revised Taxonomy.

Level of Knowledge	Course-Based Assessment Formats	Programmatic-Based Assessment Formats
Remembering Ask questions, use prompts, or develop assignments/assessments that require students to recall, repeat, or reproduce specific information.	*Quantitative exams* Students respond to true-false or multiple choice questions or match items from two lists. *Assignment* Students write summaries of course readings or class lectures.	*Direct* Reflection paper (Ask the students to summarize the program/event.) *Indirect* Postprogram student survey, program review data (Ask the students about specific information they should have learned at the program/event.)
Understanding Ask questions, use prompts, or develop assignments/assessments that require students to describe or discuss specific information or topics.	*Qualitative exams* Ask the students to provide an example. *Assignment* Ask the students to summarize key concepts or ideas in their own words (in-class or take-home assignment).	*Direct* Reflection paper (Ask the students to describe what they learned at the event and how their view on the topic changed after attending the program/event.) *Indirect* Postprogram student survey, focus group interviews, program review data (Ask the students questions about whether their understanding of the topic changed as a result of attending the event.)

Figure continued page 24

Figure continued from page 23

Level of Knowledge	Course-Based Assessment Formats	Programmatic-Based Assessment Formats
Applying Ask questions, use prompts, or develop assignments/assessments that require students to illustrate specific information or to solve a problem.	*Assignment* Students apply a well-known procedure to a problem; student must find a solution to an unfamiliar problem (lab or take-home assignment).	*Direct* Reflection paper, e-portfolio, pass rates or scores on licensure or certification tests (Ask the students to self-evaluate their skills gained and used based on the information presented during the event/program, e.g., "As a result of this lecture, I can apply…") *Indirect* Pre- and postprogram student surveys, focus group interviews, program review data (Use questions that gauge whether the student's ability to apply the information/concept increased.)
Analyzing Ask questions, use prompts, or develop assignments/assessments that require students to compare, examine, or test specific information or topics.	*Assignment* Students determine the most important parts of information provided, construct an argument of how the author came to hold a particular position or reached a certain conclusion, or connect information to other concepts learned in the course (take-home assignment or class discussion).	*Direct* Reflection paper, e-portfolio (Ask students to explore who might benefit from this kind of program and the kinds of benefits they are likely to receive from participating.) *Indirect* Pre- and postprogram student surveys, exit interview, program review data (Use questions that gauge whether the student's ability to analyze the information/concept increased.)

Figure continued page 25

Figure continued from page 24

Level of Knowledge	Course-Based Assessment Formats	Programmatic-Based Assessment Formats
Evaluating Ask questions, use prompts, or develop assignments/assessments that require students to evaluate, appraise, or judge specific information or topics.	*Assignment* Students critically examine the information presented by detecting inconsistencies or logical flaws, evaluate proposed solutions or hypotheses, and determine the best method to solve the problem (take-home assignment, class discussion, or group project).	*Direct* Reflection paper, e-portfolio (Ask the student to critique the information provided or activities conducted.) *Indirect* Pre- and postprogram student surveys, exit interview, program review data (Use questions that gauge whether the student's ability to evaluate the information has increased.)
Creating Ask questions or use prompts that require students to construct, design, or develop a project related to a specific topic or area.	*Assignment* Students develop a solution to a problem (long-term, cumulative take-home assignment or group project). *Cumulative assignment* E-portfolio, capstone projects, senior theses, exhibit, performances	*Direct* Reflection paper (Ask the students to design something that requires a synthesis of the information/topics.); postevent report (For student-run programs, ask students to complete a postevent report or evaluation that describes the process and challenges of planning the event or program.) *Indirect* Postprogram student survey, exit interview, program review data (Ask the students about their preparedness to synthesize all the information/topics in a cohesive manner.)

Figure 6. Examples of how to assess a learning outcome. (Anderson & Krathwohl, 2001; Center for Teaching Excellence, 2009; Miami Dade College, 2004; Skidmore College, 2009)

Questions for Reflection and Practice

Which assessment materials will complement the learning outcome and level of knowledge to be achieved (see Figure 6)?

Example **Accounting 101:** Take-home assignment that requires students to analyze a monthly accounts-payable-and-receivables transaction report and prepare an end-of-month financial report

Community Service: Focus group asking participants to reflect on what they learned about themselves and the community (e.g., their ability to contribute to the larger community, the role they play as active citizens of the world, the privilege they may have in society, the needs of the local community) as a result of participating in the day of service

___

How will I know that my assessment results are useful or meaningful? Briefly describe the assessment method and plan for collecting data.

Example **Accounting 101:** A quantitative survey of all 600 students enrolled in the course; a focus group with 10 students

Community Service: Focus group facilitated by a professional staff member who planned and attended the day of service

___

"The greatest risk... is to have no assessment results at all, thus depriving [educators] of systematic and accurate information necessary for good decisions and policies" (Schuh, Upcraft, & Associates, 2001, p. xvi).

How do I plan to use the assessment results? To improve my teaching or facilitation? To provide feedback to students so that they improve their performance in the classroom or program?

Example   **Accounting 101:** To gauge the effectiveness of teaching methods in helping students understand the material and to identify additional learning activities for the course

Community Service: To gauge the effectiveness of the reflection portion of the event and identify possibilities for improving or restructuring this event

_____

_____

_____

Concluding Thoughts

Learning can occur anywhere, with or without the articulation of measurable outcomes; however, learning is most successful and teaching or facilitation can only be improved through the use of learning outcomes. The development and assessment of learning outcomes provides a foundation to justify educational practice and the larger impact of higher education on students. We hope this guide has helped you reflect on how you assess student learning both in and outside the classroom. Yet, we recognize that this is a starting point, and we encourage you to share it with your colleagues and begin a department and/or campus dialogue about how you can more clearly articulate and assess student learning outcomes both in and beyond the classroom.

Assessment Resources

The list of resources on assessment is wide-reaching and seemingly limitless. Here, we have highlighted a handful of useful resources for practitioners who are interested in learning more about how to develop and assess meaningful learning outcomes.

Periodicals

Assessment, SAGE Publications
Assessment Journal, International Association of Assessing Officers
Assessment Update, Jossey-Bass
Journal of Assessment and Evaluation in Higher Education, Taylor & Francis
Journal of Assessment in Education: Principles, Policy and Practice, Taylor & Francis

Online Resources

American Association of Colleges and Universities VALUE (Valid Assessment of Learning in Undergraduate Education) Project, http://www.aacu.org/value/

First-Year Assessment Listserv (series of invited essays on assessment practice in the first college year), http://sc.edu/fye/resources/assessment/index.html

References

Anderson, L. W., & Krathwohl, D. R. (Eds.). (2001). *A taxonomy for learning, teaching, and assessing: A revision of Bloom's taxonomy of educational objectives.* New York: Addison Wesley Longman.

Astin, A. W. (1993). *Assessment for excellence: The philosophy and practice of assessment and evaluation in higher education.* Phoenix: The Oryx Press.

Baxter Magolda, M. B. (1992). *Knowing and reasoning in college: Gender-related patterns in students' intellectual development.* San Francisco: Jossey-Bass.

Bloom, B. (Ed.). (1956). *A taxonomy of educational objectives: The classification of educational goals: Handbook 1, The cognitive domain.* New York: David McKay Company.

Bosland, J. (2007). *Measuring student learning in the co-curriculum: A toolbox.* La Cruces, NM: New Mexico State University. Retrieved October 30, 2009 from http://cel.nmsu.edu/assessment/files/TA%20Measurement%20Tools.ppt

Bresciani, M. J., Zelna, C. L., & Anderson, J. (2004). *Assessing student learning and development.* Washington, DC: NASPA.

Center for Teaching Excellence. (2009). *7 things about learning outcomes*. Columbia, SC: University of South Carolina. Retrieved September 3, 2009, from http://www.sc.edu/cte/learningoutcomes/index.shtml

Chickering, A. W., & Reisser, L. (1993). *Education and identity* (2nd ed.). San Francisco: Jossey-Bass.

Cross, W. E., Jr. (1991). *Shades of black: Diversity in African-American identity.* Philadelphia, PA: Temple University Press.

Hannah, L. S., & Michaelis, J. U. (1977). *A comprehensive framework for instructional objectives: A guide to systematic planning and evaluation.* Reading, MA: Addison-Wesley.

Hauenstein, A. D. (1998). *A conceptual framework for educational objectives: A holistic approach to traditional taxonomies.* Lanham, MD: University Press of America.

King, P. M., & Kitchener, K. S. (1994). *Developing reflective judgment: Understanding and promoting intellectual growth and critical thinking in adolescents and adults.* San Francisco: Jossey-Bass.

Komives, S. R., & Shoper, S. (2004). Developing learning outcomes. In R. P. Keeling (Ed.), *Learning reconsidered 2: Implementing a campus-wide focus on the student experience* (pp. 17-42). Washington, DC: American College Personnel Association, Association of College and University Housing Officers – International, Association of College Unions International, National Academic Advising Association, National Association for Campus Activities, National Association of Student Personnel Administrators, and National Intramural Recreational Sports Association.

Marzano, R. J., & Kendall, J. S. (2008). *Designing and assessing educational objectives: Applying the new taxonomy.* Thousand Oaks, CA: Corwin Press.

Miami Dade College. (2004). *Indirect measures of student learning.* Retrieved August 1, 2009, from http://www.mdc.edu/planning_and_effectiveness/Public_files/Indirect%20Measures%20of%20Student%20LearningR2.pdf

Overbaugh, R., & Schultz, L. (2008). *Bloom's taxonomy and pyramid chart.* Retrieved April 14, 2008, from http://www.odu.edu/educ/roverbau/bloom/blooms_taxonomy.htm

Perry, W. G. (1970). *Forms of intellectual and ethical development in the college years: A scheme.* New York: Holt, Rinehart, and Winston.

Schuh, J. H., Upcraft, M. L., & Associates. (2001). *Assessment practice in student affairs: An application manual.* San Francisco. Jossey-Bass.

Skidmore College. (2009). *Assessment at Skidmore College.* Retrieved March 10, 2009, from http://cms.skidmore.edu/assessment/Handbook/direct-v-indirect-assessment.cfm

Upcraft, M. L., & Schuh, J. H. (1996). *Assessment in student affairs: A guide for practitioners.* San Francisco. Jossey-Bass.

About the Authors

Jimmie Gahagan

Jimmie Gahagan currently serves as assistant vice provost for Student Engagement at the University of South Carolina-Columbia, where he also teaches a University 101 class for first-year student success. He has presented and published widely on such topics as residential learning initiatives, the first-year experience, academic advising, leadership development, the sophomore year experience, spirituality, and student retention. He has a BA in political science from the University of Richmond, a MA in Higher Education and Student Affairs, and a PhD in Educational Administration both from the University of South Carolina.

John Dingfelder

John Dingfelder was formerly a residence hall director (RHD) at Georgia State University in Atlanta. As an RHD, he was responsible for the residential curriculum and supervision of the RAs. He also advised the Hall Council and adjudicated Community Living Standards violations. John received his BS from the Pennsylvania State University and his MEd in Higher Education and Student Affairs from the University of South Carolina.

Katharine Pei

Katharine Pei currently serves as the coordinator for Leadership Development in Campus Life and Event Services at Southeast Missouri State University where she oversees student organizations and leadership programming. She earned her BS from Saint Louis University and MEd in Higher Education and Student Affairs from the University of South Carolina-Columbia.